MAYDAY! MAYDAY!

A Coast Guard Rescue

CHRIS L. DEMAREST

Margaret K. McElderry Books

NEW YORK · LONDON · TORONTO · SYDNEY · SINGAPORE

For the men and women of the USCG
and their selfless dedication to serving the public.
Semper Paratus; always ready.

With special thanks to the USCG Air Station Cape Cod
for opening all their doors to me and giving me the opportunity
to experience a part of their daily lives.
—C. L. D.

Margaret K. McElderry Books
An imprint of Simon & Schuster Children's Publishing Division
1230 Avenue of the Americas, New York, New York 10020

Book design by Abelardo Martínez
The text for this book is set in HTF Champion.
The illustrations are rendered in pastels.

Manufactured in China
2 4 6 8 10 9 7 5 3 1
Library of Congress Cataloging-in-Publication Data
Demarest, Chris L.
Mayday! mayday! : a Coast Guard rescue / Chris L. Demarest.—1st ed.
p. cm.
Summary: Rhyming text and illustrations show how the United States Coast Guard
uses aircraft and a rescue swimmer to respond to a call for help.
ISBN 0-689-85161-8 (hardcover)
1. United States. Coast Guard—Search and rescue operations—Juvenile literature. 2. United States.
Coast Guard—Aviation—Juvenile literature. [1. United States. Coast Guard—Search and rescue operations.
2. United States. Coast Guard—Aviation. 3. Rescue work.] I. Title.
VG53.D46 2004
363.12'381'0973—dc21
2002010924

FIRST
EDITION

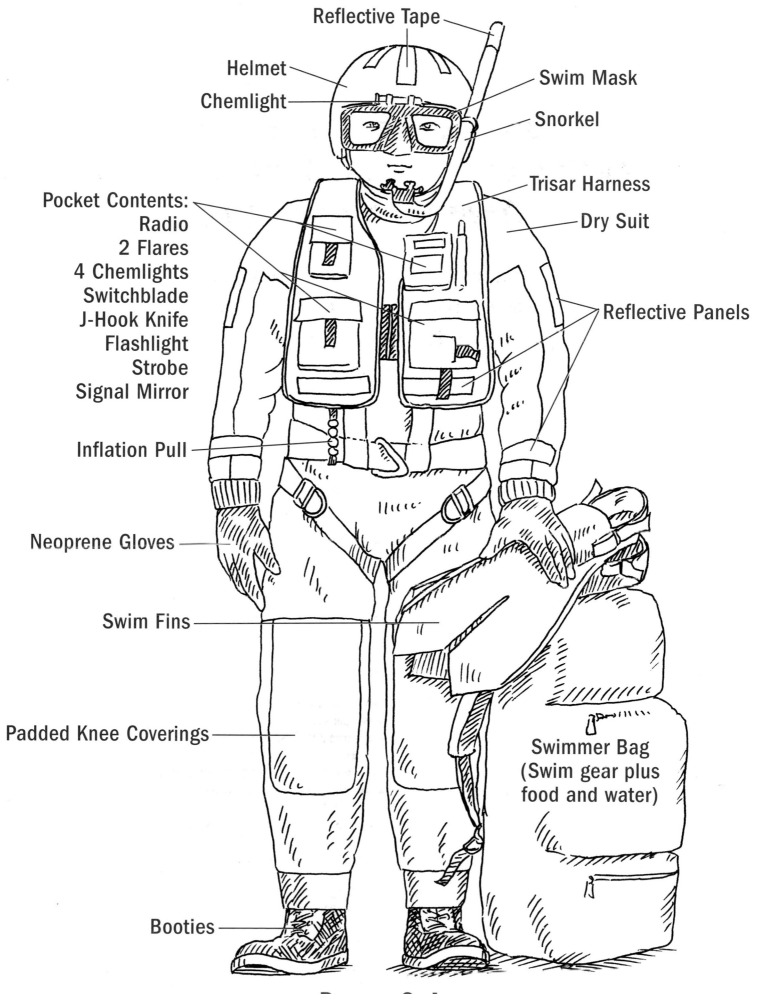

Reflective Tape

Helmet

Chemlight

Swim Mask

Snorkel

Pocket Contents:
Radio
2 Flares
4 Chemlights
Switchblade
J-Hook Knife
Flashlight
Strobe
Signal Mirror

Trisar Harness

Dry Suit

Reflective Panels

Inflation Pull

Neoprene Gloves

Swim Fins

Padded Knee Coverings

Swimmer Bag
(Swim gear plus
food and water)

Booties

Rescue Swimmer

A thirty-foot yacht, adrift well out to sea,
sends, "MAYDAY! MAYDAY! Please respond to our plea!"

The call is received at the Coast Guard air base.
An H-60 'hawk has been fueled for the chase.

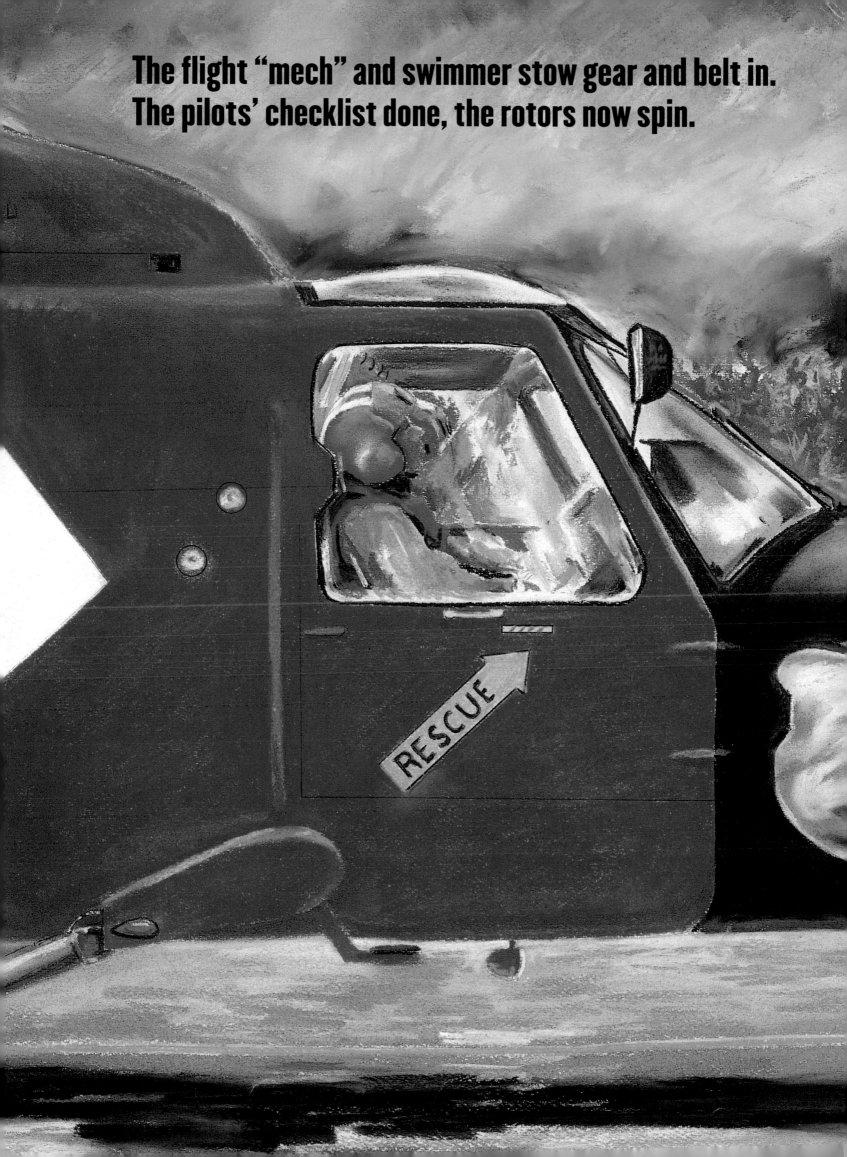

The flight "mech" and swimmer stow gear and belt in.
The pilots' checklist done, the rotors now spin.

RESCUE

In minutes, twin turbines drown out any sound.
A short taxi and then wheels lift off the ground.

The yacht, with sails reefed, gets knocked on its side.
Then righted, it battles a frightening ride.

On radar, the small boat appears dead ahead.

Then a flare lights the sky a shimmering red.

With winds steadily whipping into a gale,
a lowered winch line could entangle the sail.

So the swimmer is tapped. He knows his job well.
Thumbs-up from the mech; he drops into the swell.

A perfect drop aids the rescue swimmer's task.
His chemlight glows brightly atop his face mask.

Battling waves, the swimmer reaches the craft,
then guides the weary sailors into their raft.

Next the flight mechanic calls, "Basket away,"
then guides the pilot through the swirling salt spray.

From the raft a sailor drops into the sea
and is guided into the basket safely.

The pilot, blind to what's happening below,
listens to the mech guiding him, steady and slow.

One by one, the sailors are hoisted aboard.
Then a last drop before the basket is stored.

The weary, cold sailors are strapped into seats
as the Jayhawk then beats a hasty retreat.

Now back at the base, parked just off the runway, the refueled Jayhawk awaits the next "MAYDAY!"

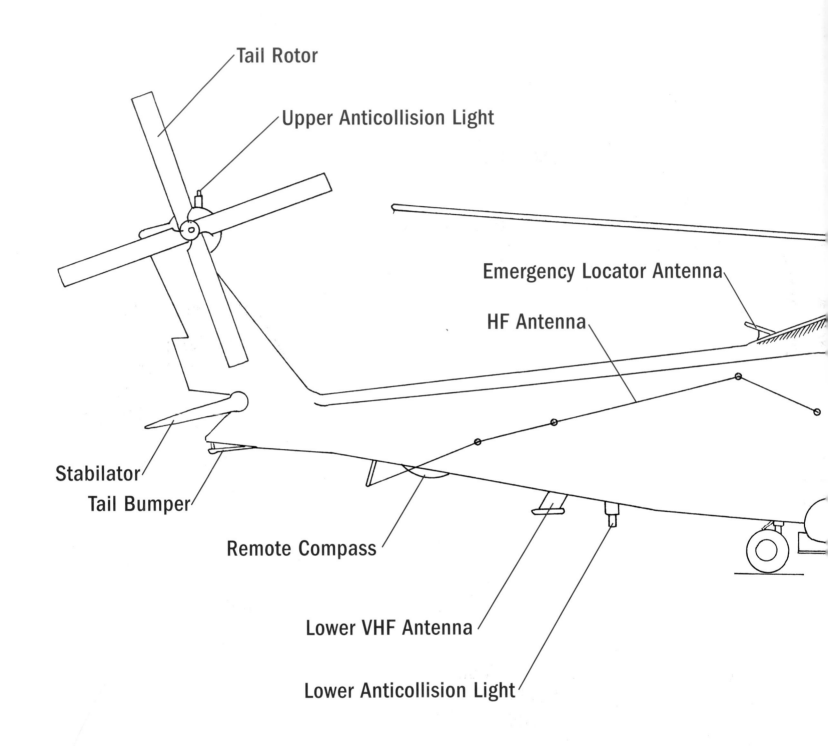

Tail Rotor

Upper Anticollision Light

Emergency Locator Antenna

HF Antenna

Stabilator

Tail Bumper

Remote Compass

Lower VHF Antenna

Lower Anticollision Light

Height to main rotor: 12 feet
Height to tail: 13 feet, 3 inches
Length overall: 64 feet, 10 inches

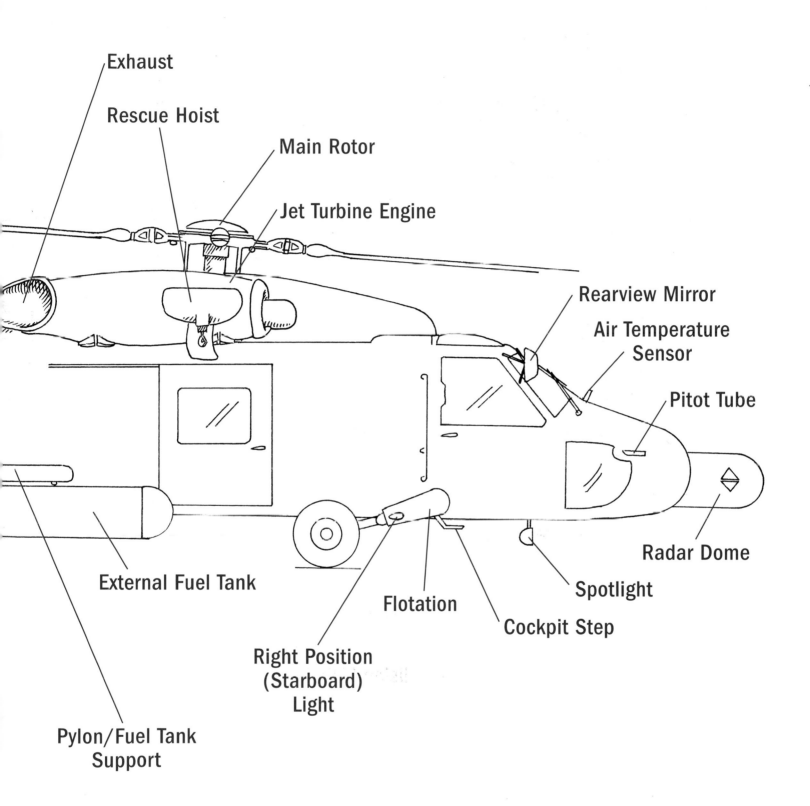

Exhaust

Rescue Hoist

Main Rotor

Jet Turbine Engine

Rearview Mirror

Air Temperature
Sensor

Pitot Tube

Radar Dome

External Fuel Tank

Flotation

Spotlight

Cockpit Step

Right Position
(Starboard)
Light

Pylon/Fuel Tank
Support

H-60 Jayhawk

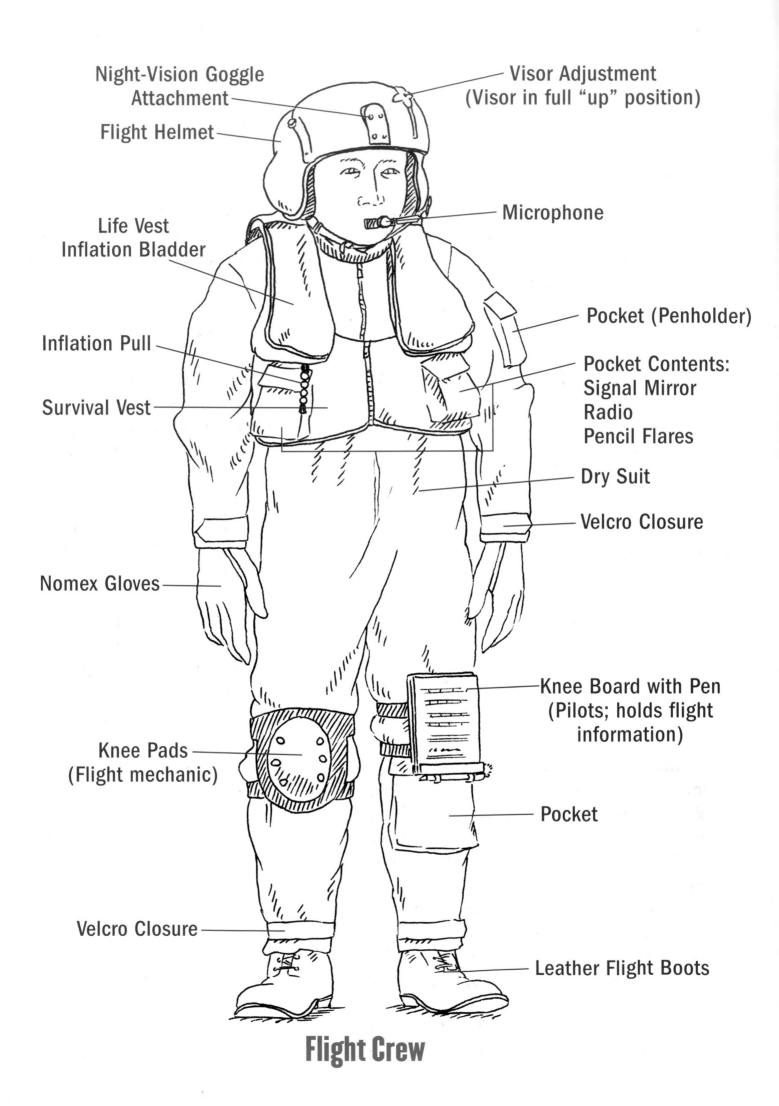

Night-Vision Goggle Attachment

Flight Helmet

Life Vest Inflation Bladder

Inflation Pull

Survival Vest

Nomex Gloves

Knee Pads
(Flight mechanic)

Velcro Closure

Visor Adjustment
(Visor in full "up" position)

Microphone

Pocket (Penholder)

Pocket Contents:
Signal Mirror
Radio
Pencil Flares

Dry Suit

Velcro Closure

Knee Board with Pen
(Pilots; holds flight information)

Pocket

Leather Flight Boots

Flight Crew

AUTHOR'S NOTE

The U.S. Coast Guard is the country's oldest maritime agency. In the late 1700s lighthouses and other navigational aids were first built by the Coast Guard to help ships safely reach one of the growing number of coastal ports. Although originally developed for the purpose of public safety on the water, the Coast Guard also took on law enforcement and later aided the U.S. Navy in war efforts. Today, with nine total districts, as far southeast as Miami, Florida, and as far northwest as Juneau, Alaska, the U.S. Coast Guard covers almost 100,000 miles of coastline, including the Great Lakes and inland waterways.

After World War II much of the focus of the Coast Guard turned back toward safety on the water. With the development of the helicopter, Search and Rescue (SAR) took a significant leap forward. People in danger could now be reached much faster than by ship, and unlike airplanes, helicopters could remove people from sinking or disabled vessels. This meant more lives were saved. The word "mayday" comes from the French term *m'aidez,* which means "Help me." "Mayday" is the accepted international call of distress.

In 1992 the H-60 Jayhawk replaced the aging HH-3F Pelican, which had been in service since the early sixties. The Jayhawk is a medium-range rotary-wing aircraft that can cover three hundred nautical miles without stopping, remain on scene for forty-five minutes, and return to shore with a total of six rescuees. If a mayday call comes far from the base, the Coast Guard will launch their faster HU-25 Falcon jet to locate the stricken craft, be it a ship or downed aircraft. They can drop supplies such as an inflatable raft, food, and water and remain on scene until the Jayhawk arrives.

A crew of four operates the Jayhawk: a pilot, copilot, flight mechanic, and rescue swimmer. Unlike in airplanes, where the pilot sits on the left, in rescue helicopters the pilot sits on the right— the same side as the hoist and rescue basket. This enables the pilot to have more visual contact with the vessel below.

When the Jayhawk arrives on scene, the flight mechanic takes over responsibilities for directing the rescue operation. Since the flight mechanic operates the hoist, which is located over the side door eight feet behind the pilot, the flight mechanic becomes the pilot's eyes in guiding the Jayhawk. To ready the rescue basket, the hoist cable is attached to the top of the basket by a large steel clip. The cable runs on a winch system, which allows the basket to be lowered and raised mechanically.

While lowering the rescue basket to the awaiting deck, the flight mechanic keeps the pilot informed of the basket's location in relation to the ship, by giving height and directional commands. In addition to concentrating on where the basket is in the air, the flight mechanic and pilot have to pay attention to the rising and falling of the vessel on rough seas to avoid any contact between the two craft.

If the seas are impossibly rough, the risk of entangling the basket in the ship's antennae or masts is greatly increased. To avoid this, a 150-foot guide rope is lowered to the ship by the cable before the rescue basket is dropped. Once the weighted end of this rope is lowered onto the deck, the helicopter backs away from the boat. The other end of the rope is attached to the top of the rescue basket, and the basket can now be lowered at a safer angle and guided onboard by the ship's crew.

The rescue swimmer, trained as an emergency medical technician (EMT), gives immediate attention on scene, when needed, before sending the patient aloft. Once a maximum of six victims and the rescue swimmer are aboard the Jayhawk and secured, the flight mechanic gives the pilot a verbal OK. The helicopter flies to the closest medical facility.

The Jayhawk is equipped with the latest navigational technology. Global Positioning Systems (GPS) give the flight crew their exact location. The flight crew is also equipped with night-vision capabilities in both goggles and Forward Looking Infrared Radar (FLIR) to enable a night rescue operation to take place more safely. There are many other automated systems that provide for approaches, hovers, and emergency departures. If a collision with a vessel or a rogue wave threatens to knock the helicopter out of the sky, a button pushed will immediately propel the craft 150 feet upward and out of harm's way.

As with all aspects of the Coast Guard, success comes down to personnel training. Years of experience go into making a team work as one. It's a dedication to saving lives that is the backbone of the U.S. Coast Guard. Those orange and white colors are there to remind the public of their motto: "Always ready."

—C. L. D.

From left to right: Emma D. Dryden, VP & Editorial Director of McElderry Books; Jim McGinley, AMT 3 Flight Mechanic; Brian Laubenstein, AST 1 Rescue Swimmer; Lt. Comdr. Mark Morin, Pilot; Lt. John Mixon, Pilot; and Chris L. Demarest, author/artist, in front of H-60 Jayhawk, U.S. Coast Guard Air Station Cape Cod